Author:

Scott Steedman grew up in Australia and Prince George, a town in Western Canada that began as a fur-trading fort. He studied natural history at the University of British Columbia, Vancouver, and has edited many books on science and history for children.

Illustrator:

Mark Bergin was born in Hastings, England, in 1961. He studied at Eastbourne College of Art and has specialized in historical reconstruction since leaving art school in 1983.

Series creator:

David Salariya is an illustrator, designer, and author. He is the founder of the Salariya Book Company, which specializes in the creation and publication of books for young people, from babies to teenagers, under its imprints Book House, Scribblers, and Scribo.

Editor: **Vicki Power**

Editorial Assistant: **Carol Attwood**

Published by SCRIBO
25 Marlborough Place, Brighton BN1 1UB
A division of Book House, an imprint of
The Salariya Book Company Ltd.

ISBN 978-1-909645-10-3

Printed and bound in China.
Printed on paper from
sustainable sources.

1 3 5 7 9 8 6 4 2

CONTENTS

A FRONTIER FORT

Written by
Scott Steedman

Series created by
David Salariya

Illustrated by
Mark Bergin

SCRIBO

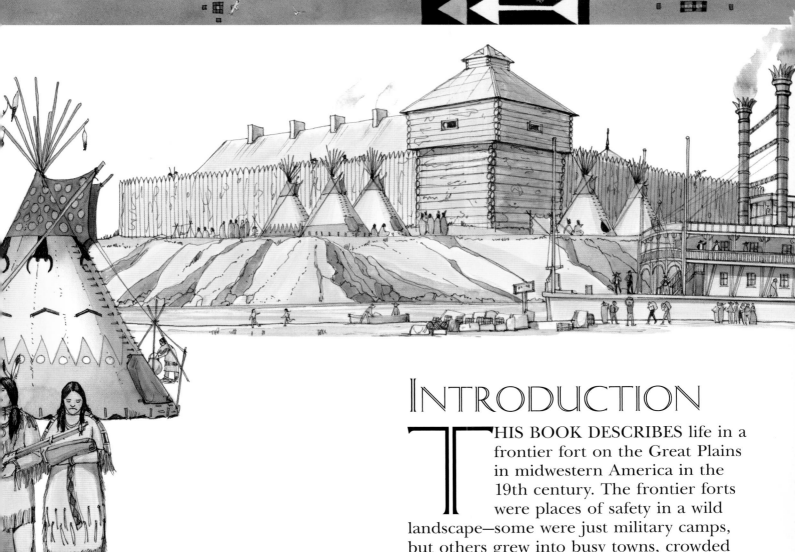

INTRODUCTION

THIS BOOK DESCRIBES life in a frontier fort on the Great Plains in midwestern America in the 19th century. The frontier forts were places of safety in a wild landscape—some were just military camps, but others grew into busy towns, crowded with trading posts and workshops. Indians, fur trappers, gold miners, and farmers brought goods to the fort to sell. Pioneers, on their way to set up new homes in the West, rested and bought provisions within the shelter of the fort's high walls.

The forts needed the protection of high walls and other fortifications. From 1492, when Christopher Columbus landed, until late in the 19th century, America was a battleground. The new arrivals, from Spain, France, Britain, Holland, Portugal, even Russia, often fought each other. They also fought the Indians, or recruited different Indian tribes to help them in battles. Then came wars between the United States of America, Britain, and Mexico, followed by the American Civil War and the Indian Wars. The frontier fort gave people a place to meet and rest in safety.

Spear

Tomahawk

Drum

Alaska

The Northwest Coast people carved huge dugout canoes and beautiful totem poles.

Totem pole

The Rocky Mountains run north–south from Alaska to Mexico. Capped with glaciers and year-round snowfields, they divide North America in two. The Rockies' high peaks are home to mountain lions, grizzly bears, and animals like bighorn sheep and mountain goats that are specially adapted to climbing steep slopes.

Elk

Wolf

Bald eagle

Harsh deserts lie beween the Rockies and the sea. They include Death Valley, one of the hottest places on Earth. The deserts are famous for their cacti, such as the giant saguaro.

Rocky Mountains

Grizzly bear

The New World

THE EUROPEAN SETTLERS called it the "New World," but really North America was just as old as Europe. In the late 1400s and 1500s, it was a land of snowy mountain ranges, dark forests, scorching deserts, and endless plains. These teemed with plants and animals, many never seen before by Europeans; grizzly bears and timber wolves, and geese soaring overhead.

In 1492, when Christopher Columbus landed in the West Indies, he was welcomed by friendly Arawak people. Thinking he had arrived in India, Columbus called them Indians.

Pacific Ocean

California

Mexico

Greenland

Inuit

Seal

Hunting knife

Pipe decorated with feathers

Arctic Ocean

Hudson Bay

The east coast forests are thick with deer and other animals. Tribes such as the Huron and Mohican hunted them with bow and arrow, and gathered wild berries and nuts.

Two mighty rivers, the Missouri and the Mississippi, cut across the plains and flow into the Gulf of Mexico. Further north, the five Great Lakes join the St. Lawrence River, which runs into the Atlantic Ocean. The cold northern rivers flow into Hudson Bay and the Arctic Ocean beyond.

Transport along rivers by birchbark canoe

St. Lawrence River

Newfoundland

Beaver

The Great Lakes

The Great Plains (right) are endless stretches of tall grass where few trees grow.

Missouri River

The Great Plains

Virginia

Buffalo

Mississippi River

Atlantic Ocean

West Indies

Gulf of Mexico

The native people of North America belong to more than 300 tribes and speak many different languages. The richest and most powerful were the Aztecs. These fierce warriors ruled most of Mexico, sacrificing thousands of people from other tribes in bloody rituals every year.

Many smaller tribes were spread across the vast areas that are now called Canada and the United States. The most famous, like the Sioux and Blackfoot, lived on the open plains, hunting deer, wolves, and buffalo. They were nomads, packing their teepees (tents) and moving camp with the changing seasons.

7

EXPLORERS AND SETTLERS

IN THE CENTURIES after Columbus's discovery, people from every country in Europe came to North America. Some were looking for a new home; others came in search of gold and silver.

Columbus had been supported by Queen Isabella of Spain and the Spanish were eager to follow his footsteps. They had heard stories of El Dorado, a country where the streets were paved with gold. They traveled up and down the west coast of North America looking for this land of treasures. By 1776, "New Spain" stretched as far north as San Francisco, California.

The Viking Leif Ericsson (above) was probably the first European to set foot on American soil.

The fortified village of Pomeiooc (below), first seen by white settlers in 1585.

The Spanish crushed the Aztecs. By 1550, Mexico was part of "New Spain."

Spanish *Conquistador,* or "conqueror."

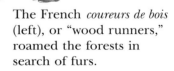

The first British settlers built Jamestown, Virginia (below) in the early 1600s. It was soon surrounded by huge tobacco plantations.

The French *coureurs de bois* (left), or "wood runners," roamed the forests in search of furs.

New Amsterdam (below) was a Dutch fort and fur-trading center. When the British captured it, they named it New York.

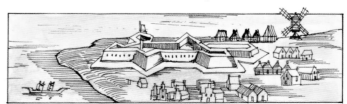

Fort Nelson, Canada (above). This was one of a string of fur-trading posts built by the British Hudson's Bay Company.

The Iroquois helped the British fight the French.

Like the majority of American towns, Charleston, South Carolina (above) began as a tiny walled village.

Forty years later (below), Charleston had grown into a bustling port visited by ships from all over the world.

The French and English fought a bloody war from 1754 to 1763 (left). The French had many strong forts, but they lost the crucial battle, on the Plains of Abraham near Quebec.

Pontiac (right), chief of the Ottawa, led a rebellion against the British in 1763.

General Hamilton (below), a British commander, surrenders Fort Sackerville to the American Colonel Clark in 1779 during the Revolutionary War.

The French set up a chain of fur-trading forts from the St. Lawrence River south to the Gulf of Mexico.

English settlers landed in Virginia and Massachusetts on the east coast. They would have starved if the local Indians hadn't shown them how to grow corn.

Two wars opened up North America. First the British beat the French, taking control of most of the land in 1763. Then in 1775, Britain's colonies rebelled. The Revolutionary War ended in 1783 with the foundation of the United States of America.

Early Forts

FOR TIRED TRAVELERS trudging through the eastern forests, Fort Harrod in Kentucky was a welcome sight. In the 1780s, its high walls protected a small community of farmers. With simple hand tools, they had cleared the land and built the fort with the timber. Almost everything was made of wood; even the "nails" were wooden pegs. A small spring inside the fort supplied all the water.

Farmers living in homesteads nearby came to the fort to grind their corn and buy supplies. Their children learned their lessons in a one-room school.

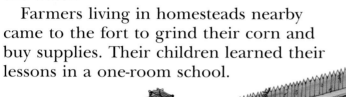

Lewis and Clark (left) were American explorers. They left St. Louis, in Missouri, in March 1804 and headed west. With the help of Sacajawea, a Shoshini Indian woman who acted as guide and translator, they traveled across the Rocky Mountains. They finally saw the Pacific Ocean in November 1805.

A "mountain man" (above) dressed in homemade buckskin clothes rides into a fort with the body of an ellk slung over his horse.

A fur trapper watches a log fort being built on the Yellowstone River (above). He is riding a half-wild Indian pony. Fur trappers were the first white men to explore the Rockies.

Like a castle in the Middle Ages, Fort Nez Percés (above) sheltered trappers in what is now known as Washington State.

The neighbors lend a hand to build a log cabin (left).

There were no roads through the forest, and the best way to travel was along the rivers by canoe (below).

Driven from their land by the new settlers, Cherokee Indians plod west on the "Trail of Tears," 1838.

Cows and pigs foraged for wild grass in clearings outside the fort. The settlers hunted deer, buffalo, and grouse for their meat, hides, and feathers.

Log cabins formed one wall of the fort. The leaders of the community lived in the bigger blockhouses at the corners. Guards with guns patrolled a raised walkway, keeping lookout for hostile Indians. The land was cleared for 100 yards (90 m) beyond the walls. This was farther than a rifle could fire accurately, giving the settlers time to react to attack.

If the fort was raided, everyone would run to shelter in the blockhouses. The stockade gates would quickly be bolted with big sliding logs.

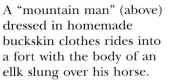

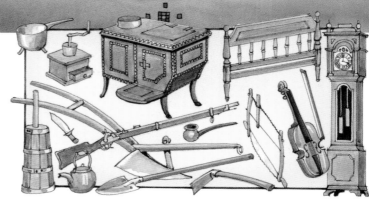

THE WAY WEST

THEIR CANVAS TOPS flapping in the wind, a long line of wagons rolls across a sea of grass. This is a wagon train making the long trek west. The wagons were nicknamed "prairie schooners." In the early 1800s, most of America was wild and unexplored. With no frontiers to stop them, brave men, women, and children packed up everything they owned, left their homes, and traveled west to make a new life there. They became known as pioneers.

They had heard stories of the wonderful farming country in Oregon and California, on the Pacific coast. But to get there, they had to cross long stretches of dry prairie and desert, then drive their wagons up steep trails over the Rocky Mountains. The grueling journey was over 2,000 miles (3,200 km) long and took from four to six months.

Long lines of wagons were less likely to be attacked by Indians. The biggest wagon trains included several hundred families, following each other in a line.

Everything needed on the journey and afterward was crammed inside the wagon. Plows and shovels, a stove, a bedstead, and a grandfather clock all had to fit in somehow. Often there was no room left for the people, who had to walk beside the wagon.

The "prairie schooners" were usually pulled by teams of oxen. The wagons had no brakes or springs, so the ride was bumpy. Oxen are very slow walkers, so 12 miles (19 km) was a good day's trek.

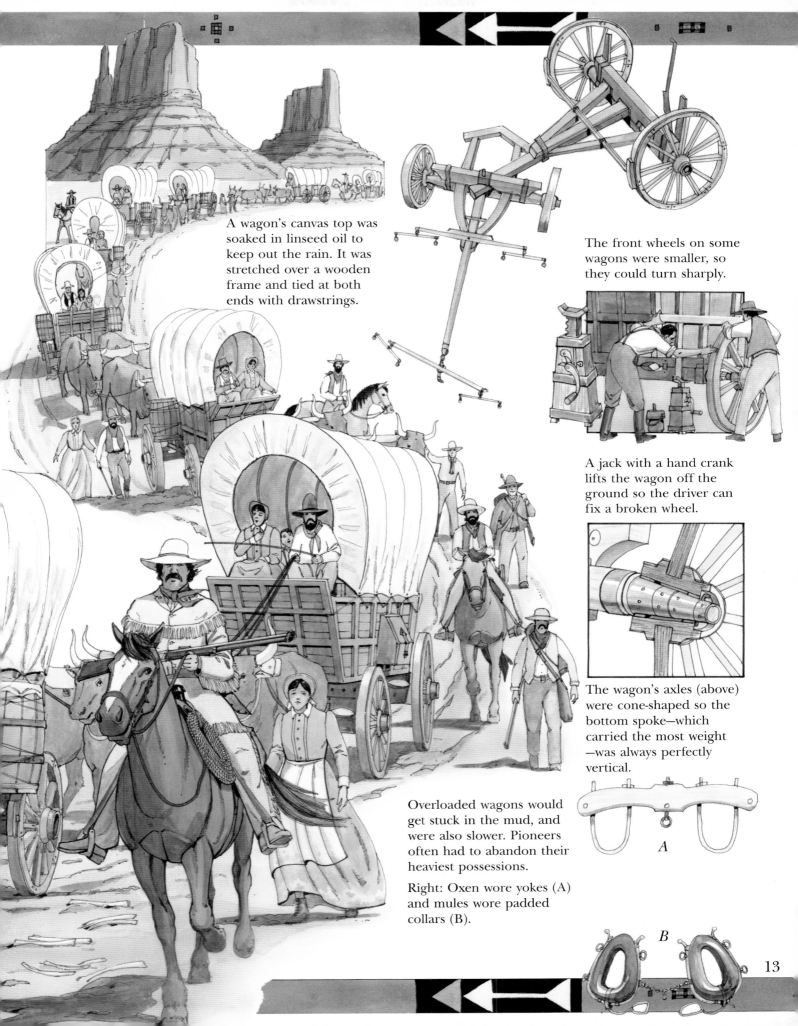

A wagon's canvas top was soaked in linseed oil to keep out the rain. It was stretched over a wooden frame and tied at both ends with drawstrings.

The front wheels on some wagons were smaller, so they could turn sharply.

A jack with a hand crank lifts the wagon off the ground so the driver can fix a broken wheel.

The wagon's axles (above) were cone-shaped so the bottom spoke—which carried the most weight —was always perfectly vertical.

Overloaded wagons would get stuck in the mud, and were also slower. Pioneers often had to abandon their heaviest possessions.

Right: Oxen wore yokes (A) and mules wore padded collars (B).

A

B

OREGON TRAIL

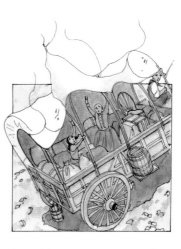

Leaving home in Boston, on the east coast, a family goes by train to St. Louis.

A steamboat then carries them up river to Independence.

The family hears the cry "Wagons, roll!" Their new wagon is fully loaded.

A sudden storm scares the oxen and blows the cover off the wagon.

I T IS MAY 1850. A young family is about to set out for the green pastures of the Oregon country. They have left their home in the old city of Boston, Massachusetts, to join a long wagon train assembling in the frontier town of Independence, on the Missouri River. Other pioneers they meet have traveled much farther, from countries such as Germany and Ireland. They are all going to follow the Oregon Trail.

In Independence, pioneers haggle over the price of a wagon and buy supplies for the long journey ahead.

The first part of the trail crosses great expanses of dusty prairie. The landscape gets drier and drier as the trail rises slowly toward the distant Rocky Mountains. Scouts ride ahead, keeping an eye on the cows and horses. A group of Indians comes down to trade some food with the settlers.

After two or three months, the route cuts across the Rockies at South Pass. Some of the travelers are gold miners, in search of fortune in California. Everyone calls them "forty-niners," after 1849, the year when gold was first found. It is fall when the pioneers finally reach Oregon.

Breakfast is over. A bugle sounds, and the wagons set out again.

Fort Laramie, a rest stop. The tired pioneers buy fresh supplies. Father trades a knife for a

deerskin with one of the Indians camped outside the fort.

A broken wheel! Fellow travelers help jack up the wagon for a quick repair.

There is no bridge over the river, so the wagons splash across.

Indians hunting buffalo stampede them past the wagon train.

As night falls, the pioneers camp in two big circles for overnight security.

A passing buffalo hunter tells stories about the trail that lies ahead.

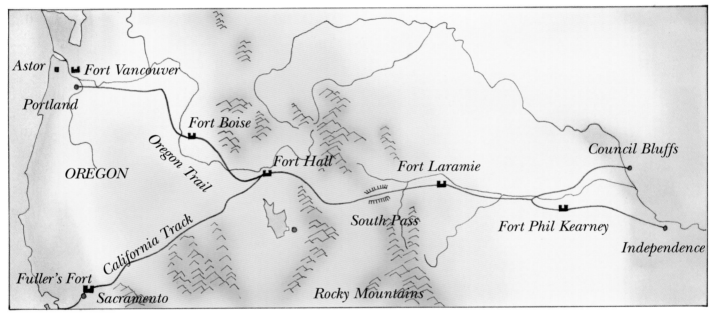

Astor

Fort Vancouver

Portland

Fort Boise

Oregon Trail

OREGON

Fort Hall

Fort Laramie

Council Bluffs

California Track

South Pass

Fort Phil Kearney

Independence

Fuller's Fort

Sacramento

Rocky Mountains

The family waves goodbye to friends going south to California.

The mountain paths are steep, and everyone has to push to help the oxen.

The wagons fan out in a dry valley. The trail is hard to find.

Oregon, at last! The wagons finally reach Fort Vancouver.

THE SITE FOR A FORT

The reconnaissance party surveys a possible site for the fort. They are looking for a flat spot on solid ground next to the river and close to the present Oregon Trail. The ideal place is a shallow bend where the river is easy to ford.

The engineer draws up a plan of the site (above).

THE U.S. GOVERNMENT wants to build a new fort along the Oregon Trail, as a safe base for soldiers to protect all the thousands of pioneers passing through each year. Army leaders consult with local trappers and an Indian agent. They decide to build the fort on a river near a buffalo range where the Sioux and Commanche Indians camp and hunt in the spring and summer.

Work begins in the spring. It is a race against the changing seasons. The days are warm now, but will the new sleeping quarters be ready before the snow comes?

Fifty soldiers and five officers arrive at the site. They make a detailed reconnaissance of the area and draw up plans. They have the river for freshwater, a forest nearby for timber, and have found limestone and sandstone to build the foundations.

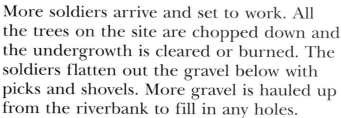

The smaller trees are felled with axes. They will be used for timber or firewood.

The dense undergrowth is cleared away with scythes, the same tools that are used to cut hay.

More soldiers arrive and set to work. All the trees on the site are chopped down and the undergrowth is cleared or burned. The soldiers flatten out the gravel below with picks and shovels. More gravel is hauled up from the riverbank to fill in any holes.

At the same time, other soldiers cut and stack dry wood to use as firewood. Eight of the soldiers are left to look after the horses.

Big trees are girdled. This means cutting away a ring of bark so that the tree slowly dies.

Firewood is then piled around the dead tree and set on fire. The huge trunk finally collapses.

A charred stump remains. The soldiers dig a pit around it, cutting the roots with axes.

A team of oxen is tied to the stump. Whipped into action, they drag it out of the ground.

The building site (below). The soldiers clear all vegetation, then break up the ground with picks and shovels. This is back-breaking work. Then teams of oxen drag harrows (heavy frames with metal teeth) up and down to level the soil.

Until the stables are built, horses are kept in a makeshift corral.

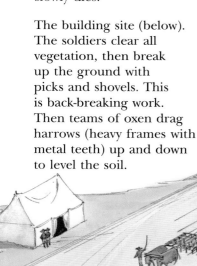

BUILDING SITE

NOW THAT THE site is level, work on the fort can begin. Companies of soldiers are busy cutting down trees. Teams of mules and oxen drag the heavy logs to the site, where the trunks are trimmed and split to make good building timber. At the biggest forts, a sawmill was built to cut timber.

The fort is rectangular. The first buildings to go up are the blockhouses. There will be three of these, two at opposite corners and a third above the main gate.

Blockhouse

Trees are felled, cut to length, and hauled to the fort (above). Big tree trunks are split in two using wedges (below).

Some logs for building are trimmed square to make them fit together neatly.

Two blockhouses and more than half the palisade wall have been built (right). The tall tree trunks that form the palisade stand side by side, their bases sunk into a ditch.

Buildings have stone foundations so that the logs will not rot. The logs are cut to length and notched at both ends. Then teams of soldiers put them in place and fit the notched ends together.

As the structure rises, the soldiers set up a log ramp to haul logs up to the top.

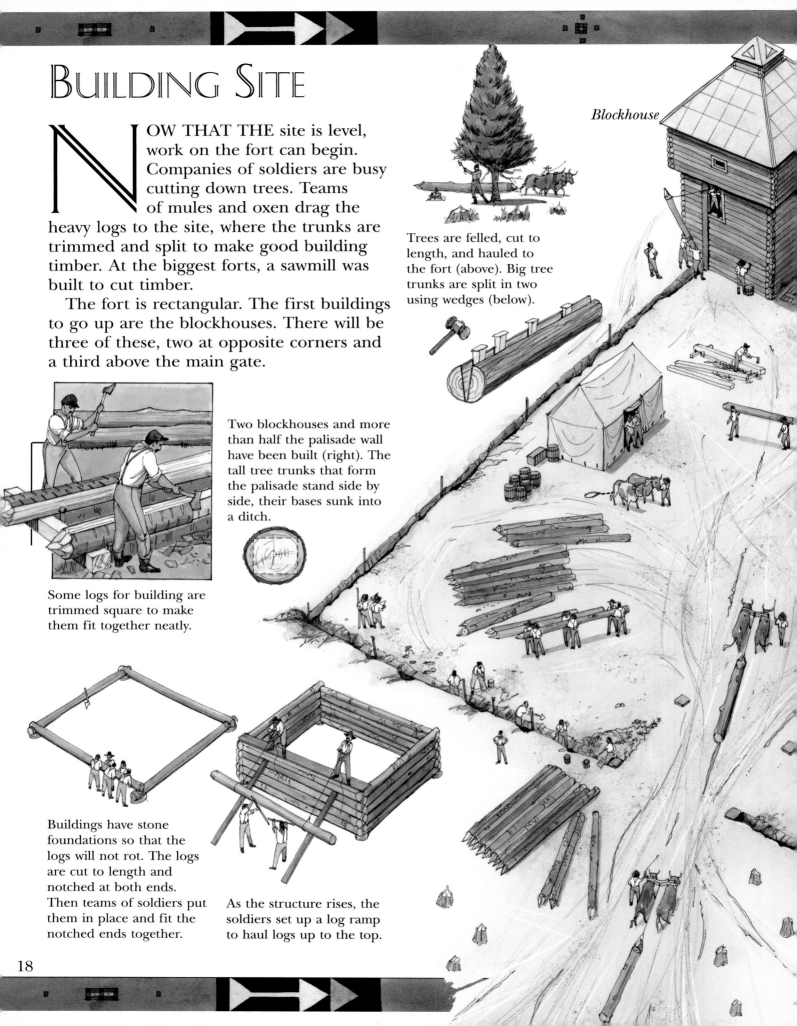

Tools to make roof-shingles:
1. Maul, to hit the froes.
2 & 3. Froes (splitting tools).
4. Drawknife.

The shingle maker (above) uses a froe, like a broad chisel, to split off slices from a large block of wood.

He smooths down one end with a drawknife. His wooden bench is called a "shaving horse."

The shingles are nailed to the roof, overlapping like tiles (above). Doors are hung in place (left). Gaps between the logs are sealed with mud or clay (below).

Palisade

Gallery

Blockhouse

The whole fort is enclosed by a palisade, a high wooden wall. It is made of tree trunks 16 feet (5 m) high, sharpened at the top and set into the earth. A raised walkway for sentries—the gallery—runs behind the palisade walls.

Many of the buildings are made of wood, but some are made of adobe—clay mixed with straw or grass. The soldiers stomp, barefoot, on the wet adobe to pack it into bricks. These take a week or two to dry in the sun. Walls of adobe bricks are finally plastered with a layer of wet clay. The word *adobe* comes from the Spanish *adobar,* which means "to plaster." Some forts are made entirely of adobe.

INSIDE THE FORT

THE FORT is finished. A company of infantrymen (foot soldiers) goes through its morning drill on the central parade ground. Two privates stand by the big gun, a 12-pound howitzer, that faces the main gate. In the stables, cavalrymen feed and brush the horses. The fort has a blacksmith and a saddler to shoe horses and mend saddles.

The soldiers' barracks, adjacent to the kitchen and messroom, are heated with woodburning stoves. All the water has to be fetched with buckets from the well.

Most of the time, the Indians camped by the fort (above) got on well with the soldiers and the many passing settlers.

In spring and summer, wagon trains of pioneers come and go. The carpenter and wheelwright are kept busy repairing wagons and wheels. Pioneers, trappers, and Indians all use the shop of the sutler, the fort's trader. They buy rice, tobacco, coffee, nails, and supplies of all kinds.

Sentries walk the walls, looking over the plains below. A band of Sioux Indians is camped just outside the wall. The Sioux come and go freely, collecting provisions and bringing furs and mocassins to exchange with the fort's sutler. They leave with pieces of colorful cloth, blankets, knives, ammunition, and bottles of whiskey.

Stables

Sioux camp

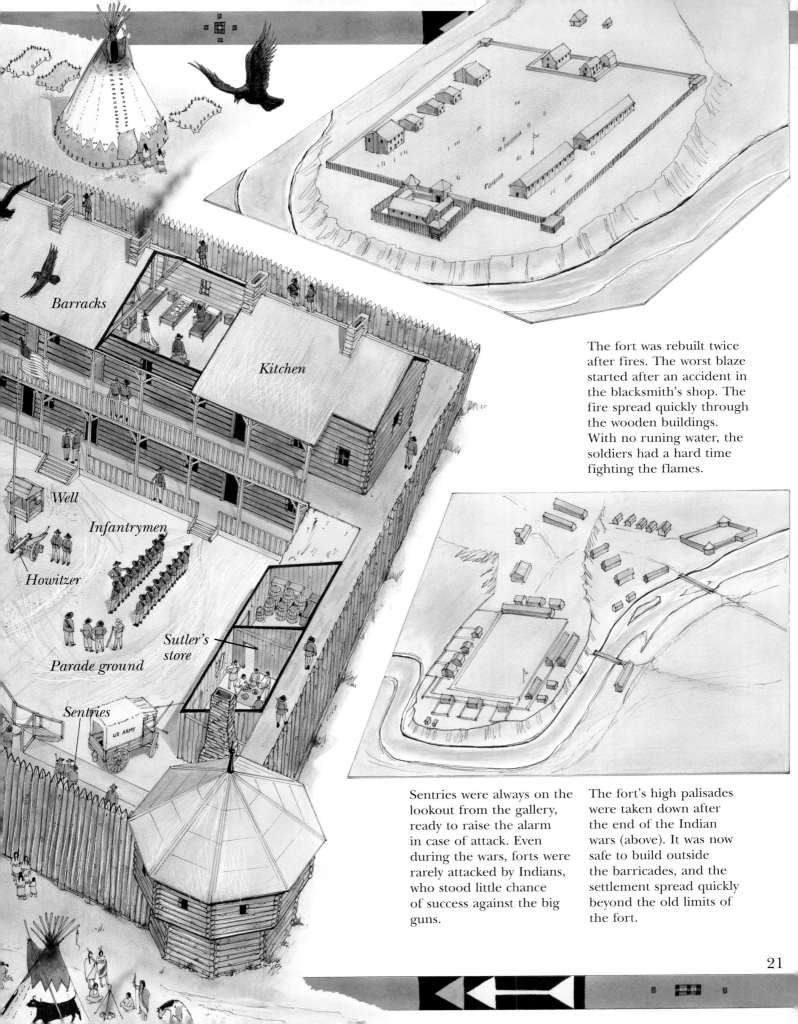

Barracks

Kitchen

Well

Infantrymen

Howitzer

Parade ground

Sentries

Sutler's store

The fort was rebuilt twice after fires. The worst blaze started after an accident in the blacksmith's shop. The fire spread quickly through the wooden buildings. With no runing water, the soldiers had a hard time fighting the flames.

Sentries were always on the lookout from the gallery, ready to raise the alarm in case of attack. Even during the wars, forts were rarely attacked by Indians, who stood little chance of success against the big guns.

The fort's high palisades were taken down after the end of the Indian wars (above). It was now safe to build outside the barricades, and the settlement spread quickly beyond the old limits of the fort.

PEOPLE OF THE FORT

Captain

General

Sergeant

Private
(infantryman)

BEING A SOLDIER in an American frontier fort was not very glamorous. The biggest forts, such as Fort Laramie, were like bustling frontier towns. But most were isolated outposts surrounded by unmapped wilderness. Life must have been very boring.

Senior officers had the most privileges, often sharing their houses with their families and servants. More junior officers could entertain friends in their private rooms, but privates (ordinary soldiers) lived together in barracks. The only women they were likely to meet were laundresses, or the general's wife! The only other civilians at many forts were Indian agents and visiting mountain men.

The captain was in charge of 25 soldiers, but the sergeant kept discipline and gave orders from day to day. He supervised drills and inspections in the parade ground. Senior officers such as generals and colonels would visit the fort from time to time, to pass on government orders, negotiate treaties with the Indians, or to plan attacks against them.

A private or regular infantryman (above). He is carrying a backpack with his coffee cup attached. This man has his rolled-up blanket on top of his backpack—some soldiers wear it across their chest.

Cavalryman on
stable duty

Cavalryman
in buckskin

Cavalryman
in uniform

Indian agent

Buffalo soldier

Indian
scout

Infantrymen wore woolen uniforms and
flannel shirts all year round. They sweated
horribly in summer, and froze through the
winter. Cavalrymen wore canvas pants, to
protect their legs when riding. All soldiers
had to pay for their own uniforms, so most
bought cheap, faded clothes at auctions.

Ordinary soldiers were not paid much,
but in a remote fort there was little to
spend money on. Skilled men made a little
extra money as barbers, blacksmiths, or
saddlers. The army paymaster visited the
fort every two months. He carried a lot of
money, so armed cavalrymen rode with him
as he drove his wagon from fort to fort.

Cavalrymen were skilled
horsemen who helped
maintain order in the Wild
West and fought in wars
against the Indians. They
wore knee-high leather
boots, and often wore
buckskin jackets instead of
the regulation blue tunics.
Many cavalrymen carried
sabers (long, curved
swords) as well as revolvers
and rifles. When they were
on stable duty, they dressd
in white canvas clothes.

The Indian scouts often
wore a strange mix of
army uniform and Indian
dress. They guided soldiers
through the wilds and
helped to trail other
Indians or find their
camps. Scouts were often
from an enemy tribe; on
the Plains, for instance,
Pawnee and Crow scouts
helped in the fight against
their traditional enemies,
the Sioux.

FEEDING THE TROOPS

ARMY FOOD was dreadful and in most forts, the soldiers took turns doing their own cooking. The staples were stew, hash (cooked meat chopped up and re-heated), baked beans, salted meat (mostly pork), potatoes, melons, and dried apples.

Meat was abundant. The surrounding plains and woods were full of game animals that could end up on a soldier's plate. Bigger forts also kept livestock and grew their own vegetables. The ranching and gardening were done by soldiers or hired help. Garden laborers were unreliable, often leaving their jobs for the gold rush in California. The problem was solved by hiring Mexican gardeners, who worked hard and had no desire to go searching for gold.

Supplies were brought in to feed the army and the constant stream of pioneers. Special wagon trains left towns on the Missouri River and crossed the plains loaded down with foodstuffs. In 1858, for instance, 775 wagons pulled by nearly 8,000 oxen left the town of Atchison, Kansas, carrying more than 3.7 million tons (3.4 million metric tons) of supplies.

Meat was hung and salted (above) to preserve it, because ice was available only in winter from the frozen lakes.

Buffalo, elk, deer, jackrabbits, and "prairie chickens" (grouse) were all hunted. Cows, pigs, and chickens were farmed.

Garden duty included digging vegetables and feeding the chickens and turkeys. Gardens were sited by a river or creek, as watering the crops was difficult on the dry plains.

Buffalo

Cow

Elk

Pig

Hot coffee and pancakes smothered in molasses or maple syrup (top left) were served for breakfast. Melons (left) grew well on the plains, and were eaten as a snack or dessert. Cornbread, made from maize flour, was eaten with main meals such as stews, hash, and "white pot"(corn flour, milk, eggs, and molasses). Another staple was hardtack—dry biscuits that tasted like cardboard. Fruit was eaten fresh, or dried.

Hardtack

Corn bread

Ordinary soldiers ate together in the canteen (above). Officers dined in the more refined atmosphere of the Officers' Mess, or if they were of senior rank, in their own houses, where servants waited at table. A lot of supplies were bought from local farmers (right), who were happy to sell their excess meat or crops to a nearby fort—it was cheaper and easier than shipping it back east. The kitchen (below) was always very busy.

A Soldier's Day

The soldier wakes at 6.30 a.m. He gets dressed, starting with long underwear called "long johns."

A quick wash helps him wake up. In summer, the men often bathe in the river at the end of the day.

Dressed and ready. Every morning the soldier soaps his socks, so they won't give him blisters.

Lined up at attention on the parade ground. The sergeant assigns today's fatigue detail.

F OR AN ARMY private, life at the fort was a dull routine. Battles were rare, and the soldiers spent most of their times marching up and down the parade ground, doing hard manual work, or trying to stay awake on guard duty.

A soldier rose early. In winter, he was often washed and dressed before the sun was up. He was then assigned a fatigue detail - the day's work - by a sergeant. Fatigue details included working in the garden or kitchen, digging ditches, building roads or buildings, chopping firewood and fetching water from the river.

The soldiers have to repair a road washed out by rain. They have to march 4 miles (6.4 km) to get there.

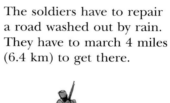

After the long march, the soldiers are digging in the hot sun by 9:00 a.m. The sergeant keeps watch.

(Left)
A private's field sack and provisions for a day away:
(1) tobacco
(2) matches
(3) razor
(4) sewing kit
(5) coffee beans
(6) onions, potatoes, bacon
(7) hardtack biscuits
(8) spare socks.
(9) tin water canteen
(10) coffee mug
(11) rolled blanket.

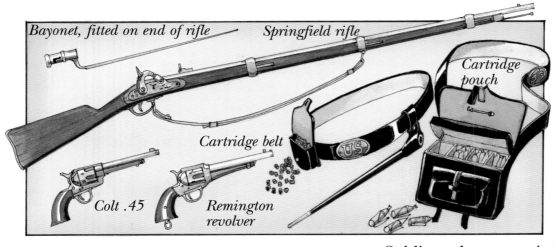

Bayonet, fitted on end of rifle — Springfield rifle

Cartridge pouch

Cartridge belt

US

Colt .45

Remington revolver

The main weapon of the Western army was the Springfield Model 1873 (left), a breech-loading .45 caliber rifle. It had a long range and was very accurate. But it had to be reloaded after each shot, unlike the repeating rifles carried by many Indians. Soldiers also carried a Colt or Remington revolver, both six-shooters.

Lunch break (below), a chance for the soldiers to relax and talk.

The march back (below). Until they reach the fort, everyone is watchful.

Soldiers always carried rations of coffee and hardtack in their backpacks. Out on patrol, they often camped and cooked far from the fort. After a day in the saddle, cavalrymen complained that it was "Forty miles a day on beans and hay."

Soldiers initially enlisted for five years; however, many deserted to try their luck at gold-panning or ranching instead. A visitor to Fort Laramie in 1850 wrote about 18 soldiers who stole the best horses in the stables and rode off to try and make their fortunes in California. A command of cavalrymen was usually sent off after the deserters, but there was always the danger that they would decide to desert too!

The sergeant gets the men to chop some wood (below) before the evening meal.

Off duty (below), the privates play baseball on the parade ground.

After dark, cards and a drink in the traders' bar. It doesn't take long to lose a week's wages!

Sentry duty starts at midnight. His body aches, and only the cold air keeps the soldier awake.

TRADERS, FURS, AND GOLD

LARGE FRONTIER FORTS were often fur-trading centers. Trappers who spent most of their lives alone in the wilds came to a fort to sell their year's furs. Traders from big companies such as the Rocky Mountain Fur Company were waiting for them. So were sutlers, who sold blankets, food, whiskey, and supplies of every kind to all the fort's visitors.

Fur traders made huge profits from the trappers, but often got even better deals by trading with the Indians. The Indians were fascinated by bright cloth and glass beads, and always wanted knives and ammunition. They had little idea of the relative value of the goods exchanged. Unscrupulous traders encouraged the Indians to depend on the fort for supplies and alcohol, so they would keep returning with furs and deerskins.

White traders followed the army as it built forts in Indian country.

This trader, in a suit and top hat, is smoking a pipe with some Sioux braves.

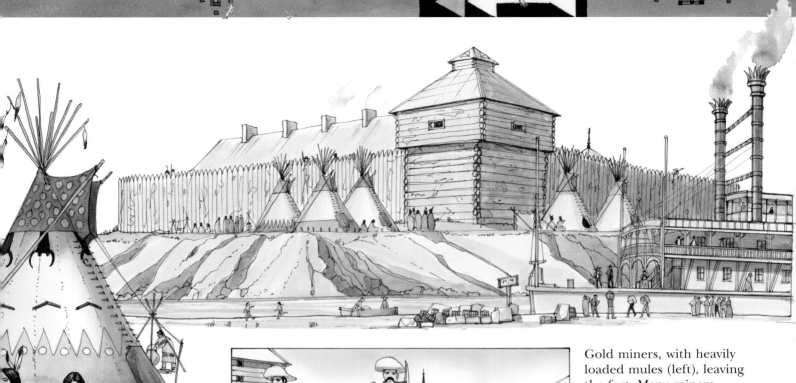

Gold miners, with heavily loaded mules (left), leaving the fort. Many miners crossed the country in search of the precious yellow metal. Most of them were badly equipped. Greedy traders made a fortune selling tools and supplies to the miners at very high prices.

Skinning a buffalo (below). By 1870, professional hunters were killing 3 million buffalo a year. Unlike the Indians, they only took the skins and tongues.

Pioneers, local farmers, gold miners, and buffalo hunters relied on the fort for news and supplies. The first prospectors were the forty-niners on their way to California; later, gold was found in other areas, such as the Black Hills of Dakota. Thousands came to the West to seek their fortunes.

The blacksmith's main job was shoeing horses, mules, and oxen. Some smiths were soldiers who mostly worked for the army. Others set up shop outside the fort. Smiths also made and mended tools such as plows for local farmers, and repaired knives and wagons for passing pioneers.

PLAINS INDIANS

After killing a buffalo, a brave thanks the Great Spirit. Then he eats the buffalo's heart to share in the animal's courage.

Plains Indians lived in teepees made of buffalo hides (below). A fire was lit inside, and a smoke flap at the top was kept open for ventilation.

An Indian woman moves camp (above). She uses the poles from her teepee to make a travois, a carrying frame which is dragged behind her horse. Her children sit on the travois, with the folded teepee cover. The woman has her baby bundled up beside her in a papoose, a deerskin pouch.

Indian agents (right) worked for the federal government, distributing any food or money promised to the Indians in treaties. Later they ran Indian reservations.

The Plains Indians often met with government and army leaders in big teepees erected outside the walls of a fort. Before a conference could begin, everyone smoked the peace pipe.

THE PLAINS INDIANS were nomadic—they moved their camps from place to place. In the summer, they set up camp near hunting grounds to follow the path of the buffalo. When the cold weather came, they packed up their teepees again and moved to a warmer winter camp, usually in a sheltered valley.

The buffalo hunt was central to Indian life. In the summer, the buffalo gathered in huge numbers. Sometimes the plains were black as far as the eye could see with thousands of dark woolly coats. When scouts located a big herd, the warriors, or braves, formed a hunting party and set off in hot pursuit. The women quickly packed up camp and followed on.

The hunters crept up, then with whoops and yells they rode through the stampeding herd, slaughtering as many buffalo as possible.

A feast of raw or roasted buffalo meat was held to celebrate the hunt. Every part of the animal was used. Hides were tanned and made into clothes, blankets, and teepee covers. Horns and bones were carved into tools and weapons. Excess meat was dried and stored for the long winter.

TRAPPERS AND TRADERS

THE FIRST WHITE people to explore the western forests were fur trappers. In the first half of the 19th century, the high demand for beaver skins brought trappers to the unmapped areas around the Rocky Mountains. The trappers were rugged men who were more at home in the wilds than in a town or farm. They became known as mountain men.

Unlike the farmers and gold miners who followed, the trappers usually lived at peace with the Indians. They adopted Indian ways, dressed in buckskin clothes and moccasin shoes, and learned Indian languages.

A mountain man's life was lonely and dangerous. The social event of the year was the "rendezvous." This was a huge gathering of trappers, Indians, and traders. The trappers came down from the mountains with their mules or packhorses loaded with furs. These were exchanged with traders for supplies and alcohol. There was singing and dancing late into the night, then the mountain men packed up and headed back to the wilds.

By 1840 beavers were rare. Many trappers became guides for government expeditions or wagon trains.

A beaver trap is chained to a wooden stake on the bottom of a stream.

When a beaver touches the bait pan, its paw is trapped in the jaws of the trap.

Bait pan

A beaver trap with jaws opened (right) and closed.

Seeing an elk in the forest, the trapper shoots it for its meat and skin.

Trappers travel by birchbark canoe. The design is an Indian one.

The canoe is carried around waterfalls. This is called a portage.

A trapper gives a bead necklace to an Indian.

Indians and trappers around the campfire.

Up to 2,000 people gather at a rendezvous.

A mountain man's Indian wife scrapes a buffalo hide (right). When it is clean of flesh, she will grease it, tan it, and stretch it out to dry. She is already drying a deerskin and some strips of buffalo meat.

Back at the campsite (above), the trapper cleans and presses his beaver skins. First he uses a metal scraper and a graining block to clean the flesh off the hide, then he packs the pelts together to make a bale. He will hope to sell all the bales at the next rendezvous.

The trapper (below, center) wears a buckskin shirt, pants, and moccasins. His mule carries some furs and a dead elk. The trapper's Hawken rifle can kill a bear from 200 yards (180 m) away.

A Pioneer's Cabin

THERE WAS LITTLE wood, stone, or clay on the plains, so many settlers made their homes from turf, or sod. Stringy grass roots in the soil held the sods together. Slabs of sod were cut from the ground with a shovel or a special plow. Then they were laid like giant bricks and the cracks were filled with earth. The walls were very thick, usually two layers wide.

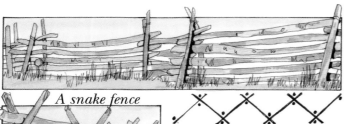

A snake fence

Before barbed wire was invented, fences were made of wood or rocks: a snake fence (above) and a rail and boulder fence (left).

Wheel

Tail

A windmill (above) pumped water from the wells deep below the dry plains. The tail kept the wheel facing the wind. Farming was almost impossible without a steady water supply.

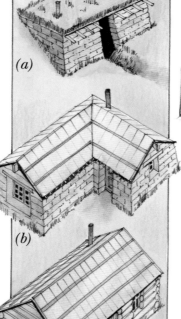

(a)

(b)

(c)

Left:
(a) The simplest sod house was cut out of a hillside. But there was always the risk of cattle falling through the roof!
(b) An L-shaped house provided more shelter.
(c) Once a farmer had saved up enough money, he could build a log cabin.

Walls two layers thick

Firewood was rare on the plains, so pioneers burned buffalo dung in their stoves. They called it "buffalo chips."

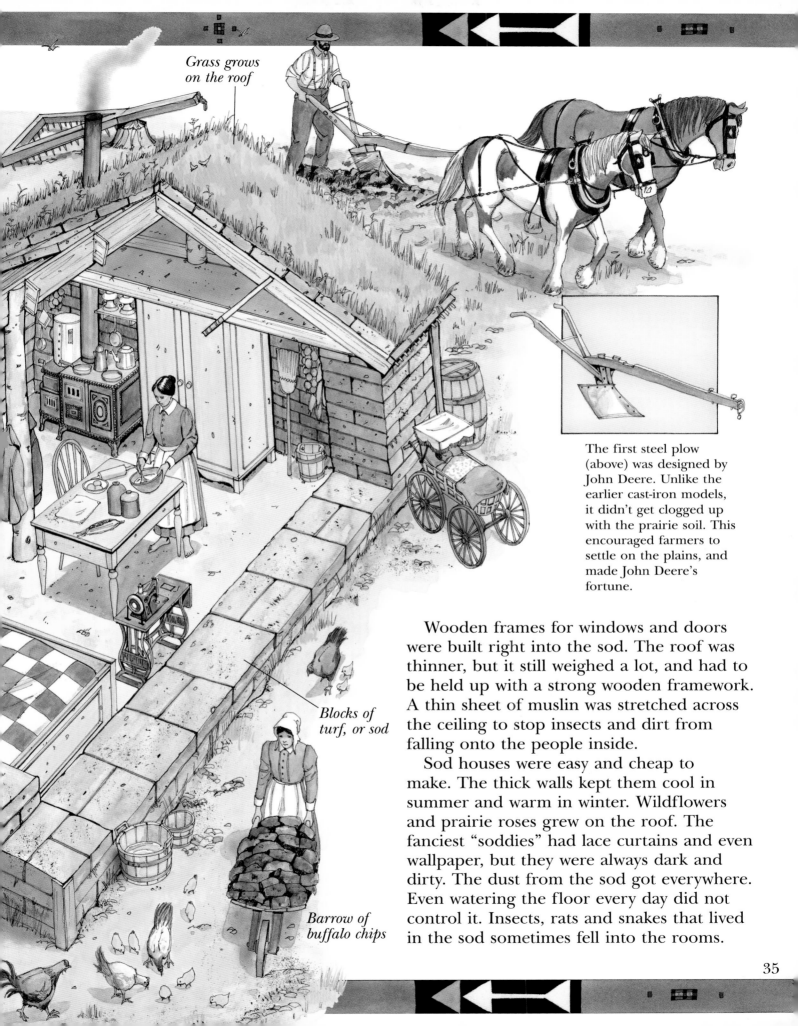

Grass grows
on the roof

The first steel plow
(above) was designed by
John Deere. Unlike the
earlier cast-iron models,
it didn't get clogged up
with the prairie soil. This
encouraged farmers to
settle on the plains, and
made John Deere's
fortune.

Blocks of
turf, or sod

Barrow of
buffalo chips

Wooden frames for windows and doors
were built right into the sod. The roof was
thinner, but it still weighed a lot, and had to
be held up with a strong wooden framework.
A thin sheet of muslin was stretched across
the ceiling to stop insects and dirt from
falling onto the people inside.

Sod houses were easy and cheap to
make. The thick walls kept them cool in
summer and warm in winter. Wildflowers
and prairie roses grew on the roof. The
fanciest "soddies" had lace curtains and even
wallpaper, but they were always dark and
dirty. The dust from the sod got everywhere.
Even watering the floor every day did not
control it. Insects, rats and snakes that lived
in the sod sometimes fell into the rooms.

A Woman's Day

FRONTIER WOMEN left the comforts of civilization behind. Running a clean and organized home was a constant struggle, and they had to be hard-working and resourceful. Women spun their own wool and flax, sewed clothes and bedding for the whole family, cooked and cleaned, and learned how to make candles from buffalo or bear fat with wicks spun from plant fibers.

The woman of the house gets up at dawn and goes to the stream to collect fresh water.

The next job is to milk the cows, which is done by hand and takes quite a long time.

The family is up and hungry for a breakfast of pancakes with molasses (a type of syrup).

Father has coffee with his breakfast and the children have fresh milk.

After breakfast the children help their mother feed the chickens and pigs with household scraps.

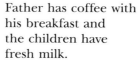

The woman tends the vegetable patch while her children pick apples in the orchard.

Some of the milk is stirred up in a churn, turning it into butter and buttermilk.

Before lunch, the woman finds time to bake some bread in her big iron stove.

She washes the family's clothes in the stream and hangs them up to dry.

The toilet: an outhouse built over a deep hole in the ground.

The woman is sewing a doll for her daughter from scraps of leftover material.

Dinner, the main meal of the day: roast turkey and vegetables and apple pie.

Neighbors help to husk the corn. They sit in the barn and talk while they work.

A few minutes' peace to patch her husband's ripped overalls.

It's been a long day, and the children are exhausted. Their mother tucks them into bed.

A quilting bee. Friends gather to sew the quilt's three layers—the top one is a colorful patchwork.

Not all women kept house. Calamity Jane (right) dressed in buckskin and liked to drink and gamble with the men. Annie Oakley (below) was a sharpshooter in Buffalo Bill's Wild West Show (see page 45).

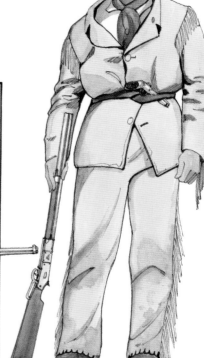

Frontier women often had six or eight children. Many women died in childbirth or lost children from diseases. It was hard to teach children about cleanliness when water had to be fetched from a stream and the main fuel was buffalo dung!

Loneliness was a problem, too—but when a family had a big job to do, like building a new barn or "swingling" (threshing) their flax crop, all the neighbors came to help. Afterward, the hostess would cook a huge meal. Then everyone would dance and sing to the sound of the fiddle.

Because they worked so hard, frontier women demanded more rights. Wyoming Territory led the way in giving women the vote in 1869, 50 years before all American women were granted that right.

BUILDING THE RAILROAD

AMERICANS DREAMED of a railroad connecting the big cities in the east with the gold-rush towns on the Pacific coast. Work began on the "transcontinental" in 1865. Two railroad companies had been granted money and land by the government for this massive project. The Union Pacific was to start at the Missouri and build a track west; the Central Pacific headed east from California to meet it.

Pony Express riders (top) carried letters to towns far from the railroad. They crossed wild territory at breakneck speed, changing horses at relay stations.

The Pony Express ended when the first telegraph line was completed in October 1861.

Laying track on the Union Pacific Railroad (left). The ties, huge pieces of rough-cut timber, were dropped across the roadbed. The "ironmen" then laid two more rails, using a gauge to keep them the correct width apart.

Chinese laborers preparing the gravel roadbed on the Central Pacific Railroad. All the laborers worked with hand tools, wheelbarrows, and horse-drawn wagons.

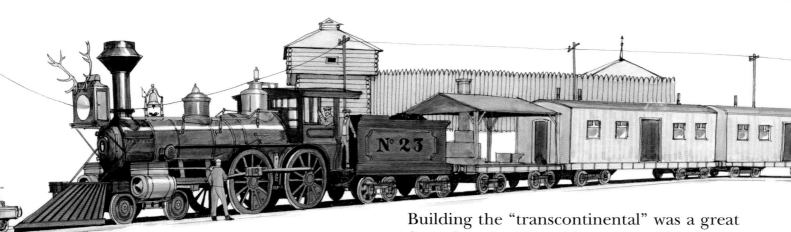

The Summit Tunnel (below) was 138 feet (42 m) long. Workers blasted away the rock from both ends and from a shaft in the middle.

A small locomotive lifted the rock from the shaft. Supplies were dragged over the mountain so work could begin there.

Building the "transcontinental" was a great feat of engineering. Thousands of men labored with picks, shovels, and gunpowder. The Union Pacific hired mostly Irish workers. Many had just arrived in America, or were veterans of the Civil War. Laying track on the plains was relatively easy but the Indians, angered by the "iron horse" invasion of their land, often attacked.

Summit Tunnel

The Central Pacific Railroad had to cross the wild Sierra Nevada mountains. The company hired more than 12,000 Chinese laborers, most of whom were brought out specially from China. They proved to be hard and fearless workers. Tunnels and bridges had to be built through cliffs and across valleys, and the work was dangerous and slow. There were no bulldozers or drilling machines, and all the work was done by hand. Hundreds of workers died in accidents or in avalanches set off by blasts.

Intricate wooden trestles (below left) carried the railroad across ravines. The timber supports for the trestles and tunnels were cut in lumber camps in the mountains.

Celebrations at last (below). On May 10, 1869, the two sections of railroad met at Promontory Point, Utah. The transcontinental railroad was 1,772 miles (2,852 km) long.

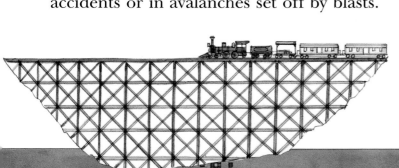

THE INDIAN WARS

The Sand Creek Massacre of 1864 (above). Soldiers attacked and killed at least 150 Cheyenne and Arapaho, mostly women and children.

Chief Joseph of the Nez Perce tribe (above) made a famous speech when he surrendered.

General George Custer (above) was a controversial Indian fighter. He was killed in 1876, in the Battle of Little Bighorn.

Sioux Chief Red Cloud (above) fought the army when they tried to build forts on Sioux land in 1865. He won, and burned the forts down.

When Chief Joseph surrendered, he said: "Hear me, my chiefs. I am tired. My heart is sick and sad. From where the sun now stands, I will fight no more forever."

Geronimo (above) was an Apache chief. For 10 years he led his small band of warriors on raids in Mexico and Arizona, escaping from prison again and again.

Sitting Bull (above) was a Sioux and one of the leaders at Little Bighorn. He fled to Canada, but eventually surrendered. He was shot dead in 1890.

T A COUNCIL OF the Nez Perce tribe in 1877, Chief Joseph said: "The White Men were many and we could not hold our own with them. We were like deer. They were like grizzly bears." The U.S. government had given his people 30 days to leave their home in Oregon and move to a reserve in Idaho. All over the frontier, the story was the same. Gold miners, farmers, and cattle ranchers were invading Indian land. They brought diseases that were unknown to the Indians. They slaughtered the buffalo and put up fences on hunting grounds.

The Indians fought many battles with the new settlers. In the 1860s the government tried to force tribe after tribe to leave their homelands and settle on reservations. Many Indians obeyed. Others chose to fight.

The Indians were brave and clever warriors. They rarely attacked the army in the open. Instead they made quick strikes or laid ambushes. But they were hopelessly outnumbered and were always running out of ammunition. The army also chose to fight in winter, when the Indians were usually settled in their winter camps. Forced to flee from the soldiers, the Indians were often defeated by the snow and cold.

Indians believed the Ghost Dance (below) would make the white man disappear. The terrible massacre at Wounded Knee in 1890, when 300 Sioux were killed, proved them wrong.

Geronimo surrendered and moved to a reservation in 1886. The picture below shows him riding in a car in 1905.

A Frontier Town

AS SETTLERS POURED into the West, bustling towns sprang up everywhere. Many forts quickly grew into cities. Shops had fake fronts to make them look bigger, and porches with hitching posts for the horses. The streets were bare earth, and the raised sidewalks were made of wooden planks. On rainy days, the wagons' wheels splattered the pedestrians with mud.

The West was full of boom towns that seemed to grow overnight. Fort Worth, Texas, was built by the army in 1849. Four years later, the town was a thriving trading center and the old fort was pulled down.

The railroad arrived in 1874, and the town was immediately overrun by cowboys and their herds of longhorn cattle. By 1885, Fort Worth had a population of 22,000.

Fort Worth was a "cowtown." Other towns boomed when the government created new states and offered cheap (or even free) land to settlers. On the morning of April 22, 1889, there were four buildings in Guthrie, Oklahoma. By nightfall 10,000 pioneers had set up their tents there. A council and mayor were elected the next day, and in a matter of weeks the town had a school, a bank, a church, and its own newspaper, called the *Get-up.*

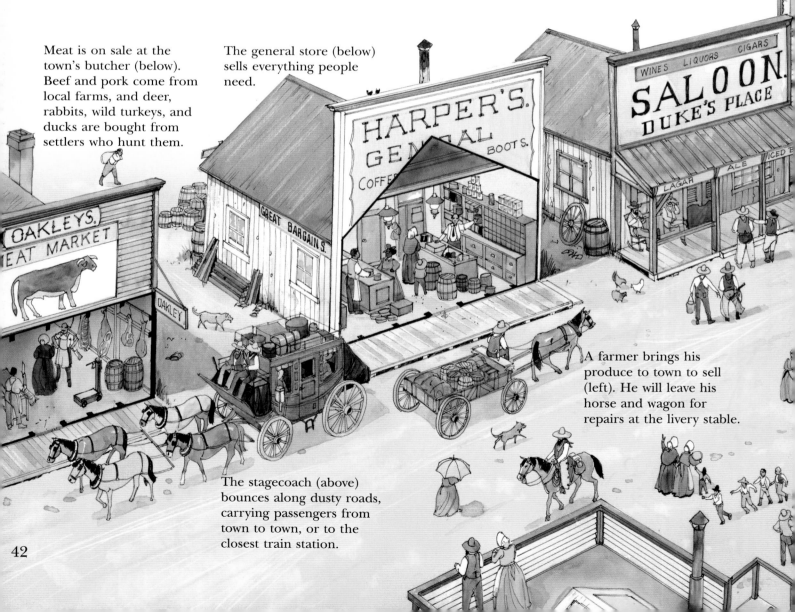

Meat is on sale at the town's butcher (below). Beef and pork come from local farms, and deer, rabbits, wild turkeys, and ducks are bought from settlers who hunt them.

The general store (below) sells everything people need.

A farmer brings his produce to town to sell (left). He will leave his horse and wagon for repairs at the livery stable.

The stagecoach (above) bounces along dusty roads, carrying passengers from town to town, or to the closest train station.

Many settlers owe money to the town bank (below). Next door, the hotel rents cheap rooms. Its inn and dining rooms are a hub of town life.

The army post, overlooking the town, is a reminder of its military origin.

Weddings, baptisms, and funerals take place in the church. Many people only come to town on Sundays for the service there.

The town's water is pumped to the surface by a tall windmill (below). Anyone can fill their buckets or refresh their horses at its trough.

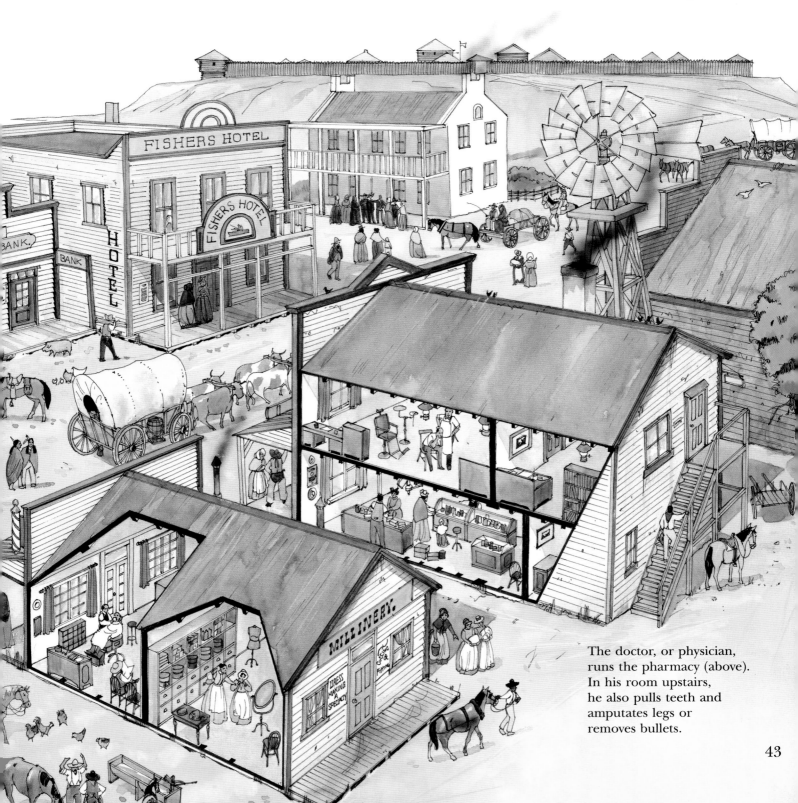

The doctor, or physician, runs the pharmacy (above). In his room upstairs, he also pulls teeth and amputates legs or removes bullets.

Fort Facts

The Alamo, a fortified mission in Mexico, was captured in December 1835 by Texans, who were revolting against Mexican rule. Two months later, a huge Mexican force took the Alamo back. They killed every defender, including Davy Crockett and James Bowie. The Texans soon defeated the Mexican army once again.

Bent's Fort had massive adobe walls. It was the biggest fort west of the Mississippi and was the center of the Colorado fur trade from 1833–1848. Pioneers on the Sante Fe Trail stopped at Bent's Fort, but most of its visitors were fur trappers, traders, or Indians.

Fort Laramie was an important stopover on the Oregon Trail in Wyoming. It was built in 1834, and soon became a major fur-trading center. In 1849, the army bought Fort Laramie and turned it into a military post. An important treaty with the Sioux was signed there in 1867.

Fort Worth in Texas is just 30 miles (48 km) from the modern city of Dallas. Built in 1849, it soon grew into a thriving trading center and city. It became a railhead in 1874.

Fort Phil Kearny was built in 1866 in the Powder River Country of Wyoming, a traditional hunting ground of the Sioux, who were outraged. Their chief Red Cloud fought a clever war against the army. He won several victories and kept the fort under seige. The army finally ageed to leave the area. Red Cloud would not sign the agreement until his warriors had burned Fort Phil Kearny to the ground.

Fort Sumter was near Charleston, South Carolina. The first shots in the American Civil War were fired there on April 12, 1861.

Fort Bridger was built by the legendary trapper and guide Jim Bridger. The fort was on the Oregon Trail by Farewell Bend, where the California trail leaves it and heads south. It was burned to the ground by angry Mormons in 1890.

Quebec City is one of the only North American cities with stone walls that are still standing. The massive fortifications, built by the French in the 17th and 18th centuries, weren't enough to defeat the British, who captured Quebec in 1759.

FAMOUS FRONTIER FOLK

Buffalo Bill Cody was a Pony Express rider, army scout, Indian fighter, and buffalo hunter. He gained the nickname "Buffalo Bill" after he killed more than 4,000 buffalo in one 18-month period. He is best known for his Wild West Shows, where real cowboys and Indians raced horses, performed riding and shooting tricks, and enacted famous battles. The show even toured Europe, and performed for Britain's Queen Victoria in 1887.

Jim Bridger was a mountain man and army guide who was the first white man to see Great Salt Lake, Utah. He established Fort Bridger in Wyoming in 1843. He married three Indian wives, and outlived them all.

Billy the Kid was a cowboy, outlaw, and murderer. In 1881, he was sentenced to death for the murder of Sheriff Brady, but he escaped from jail by killing two guards. He was eventually shot dead by Pat Garrett, an old friend who had become sheriff of Lincoln County.

Cochise was an Apache chief who fought a long war with the army in Arizona. He finally surrendered in 1871.

Crazy Horse was a Sioux warrior. He set a trap for the army in 1866, when his braves killed more than eighty soldiers in the Fetterman Massacre. He was also one of the Indian leaders at Little Bighorn. Unlike other Indian leaders, he never allowed photographers to take his picture. He was killed by a soldier in 1877.

Kit Carson was a trapper, guide, soldier, and Indian fighter. He fought in the Mexican War and the Civil War, and then led ruthless campaigns against the Apache, Navajo, Kiowa, and Comanche. He died in 1868, after a fall from a horse.

Wild Bill Hickok was a gunfighter and sheriff. He claimed to have killed over a hundred men, but he was probably exaggerating. He survived several public shoot-outs, but was finally shot in the back and killed in 1877.

Annie Oakley was a crack shot and one of the stars of Buffalo Bill's Wild West Show. She could hit coins thrown in the air, and once shot a cigarette from the lips of the German Crown Prince. Sitting Bull called her "Little Sure Shot."

GLOSSARY

Adobe Built with sundried bricks of clay and straw. Adobe walls are then plastered.

Barracks A building where soldiers sleep.

Bayonet A long blade fitted to a rifle.

Beaver A large rodent that lives in the water. Beavers were prized for their fur, which was made into fashionable hats.

Blockhouses Two-story buildings that form part of the wall of a fort.

Brave A young Indian warrior.

Buck A male deer. The skin of a buck used to be worth one dollar, or a "buck."

Buckskin Tanned deer hide used to make clothes like buckskin jackets and moccasins.

Buffalo A large wild ox with thick, dark fur. Buffalo once roamed the plains in huge herds. The correct name is American bison.

Buffalo soldier The name given to a black soldier by Indians.

Colt A famous gun manufacturer. The Colt .45 was one of the most common revolvers on the frontier.

Conquistadores The Spanish "conquerors" or soldiers who invaded South and Central America in the 16th century. They destroyed the Aztec, Mayan, and Incan civilizations.

Coureurs de bois French "wood runners" who collected furs in the northern forests. They got on well with the Indians.

Detail A soldier's special task or duty.

Elk A large deer with impressive antlers.

Fatigue A non-military duty for a soldier.

"Forty-niners" Gold miners who rushed to California in 1849 hoping to find fortune.

Frontier The wild lands to the West in 19th-century America. The frontier kept moving farther west as settlers fenced and farmed the land and cities grew.

Gallery A raised walkway inside the palisade of a fort, from which sentries can keep watch.

Gauge The width of a railroad track; also, a tool for measuring this.

Grouse A plump bird that can barely fly. Grouse are very good to eat, and were often called "prairie chickens."

Howitzer A large, powerful gun moved around on wheels.

Indian agent A government worker who distributed supplies to Indians and dealt with their complaints.

Messroom An army dining room.

Moccasins Shoes made of tanned deer or moose hide.

Molasses Thick, sugary syrup. Also called treacle.

Mule A cross between a horse and a donkey.

Officers' mess A special dining and living room for army officers.

Ox A large, strong type of cattle used for heavy work such as pulling wagons.

Palisade A high wooden wall made of upright logs.

Papoose An Indian buckskin pouch for a baby. The papoose was carried on a person's back or strapped to a horse.

Pioneer A settler in the Wild West.

Portage Carrying a boat around rapids or a waterfall or between two rivers.

Prairies The flat grasslands that cover large expanses of the West.

"Prairie schooner" A covered wagon.

Private A common foot soldier of low rank.

Reconnaissance A detailed survey of an area, usually conducted by an army.

Reservation An area set aside for Indians to live in. Many reservations are on poor land.

Revolver A small gun held and fired with one hand.

Sawmill A factory where logs are cut up into lumber.

Scouts Guides who helped travelers or soldiers find their way around or locate Indian camps. Many scouts were Indians or retired mountain men.

Sentry A soldier ordered to keep guard on a fort or expedition.

Shingles Large wooden roof tiles.

Spoke A supporting rod that runs from the hub to the rim of a wheel.

Stampede A sudden scattering of horses, buffalo, or other animals.

Sutler A fort trader.

Teepee A portable tent. The Plains Indians made teepees from buffalo hide; the Northeast tribes used tree bark.

Totem pole A log, carved with faces and animals, put up in front of a house. The Indians of the Northwest coast still make totem poles.

Travois A wooden carrying frame dragged by a horse or dog. Indians made their travois from the main posts of their teepees.

Trestle A bridge made from an intricate wooden framework.

Wagon train A big group of wagons traveling together, usually in single file.

Well A hole in the ground from which water is lifted or pumped.

Yoke A wooden collar fitted over the neck of a working animal like an ox.

INDEX

Page numbers in bold refer to illustrations.